In Deep

For Bernard
— best wishes —
Matt
May
2006

IN DEEP

MATT SIMPSON

Matt Simpson (signature)

Shoestring Press

Typeset and printed by Q3 Print Project Management Ltd, Loughborough, Leics
(01509) 213456

Published by Shoestring Press
19 Devonshire Avenue, Beeston, Nottingham, NG9 1BS
(0115) 925 1827
www.shoestringpress.co.uk

First published 2006
© Copyright: Matt Simpson
The moral right of the author has been asserted.
ISBN-13: 978 1 904886 28 0
ISBN-10: 1 904886 28 0

Shoestring Press gratefully acknowledges financial assistance from Arts Council England

For there are very good reasons for living on earth
but what we need is the strength trees have
in order to push it back up – the low sky
that death has pressing on our eyelids.

Lucien Becker trans. Christopher Pilling

…my object…is to write true things, significant
things, in words each of which works for its place
in the line.

Keith Douglas in a letter to J.C. Hall

for Monika

ACKNOWLEDGEMENTS

are due to the editors of the following publications in which
some of these poems first appeared:

The Argotist online, Contact, Critical Survey, Dream Catcher,
First Thursday Poets, Orbis, *Paging Dr Jazz* (Shoestring Press),
poettext.com, The Reader, The Review of Contemporary Poetry,
Smoke, Stride online.

A version of *The Day We Saw Dolphins* appeared in the
chapbook *Somewhere Down the Line*, Shoestring Press, 1998;
And Once at Lumb Bank appeared in a different form in
The Way You Say the World: a Celebration for Anne Stevenson,
Shoestring Press, 2003. The *Prelude* to the *November Song*
sequence is a re-writing of one that appeared in the pamphlet
Letters to Berlin, Driftwood Publications, 1971;
earlier versions of *Reported Missing, Tending, Clearing Out* and
That Old Feeling were printed in *Catching Up With History*,
Bloodaxe Books, 1995.

Casting Off and *Out There* were broadcast on BBC Radio
Merseyside.

CONTENTS

I

II

I

CASTING OFF

For the kind of making I'm used to
these left-over skeins of brown,
tucked too long
in the clutter of the drawer, will do.

Holding them as if they were
bundled hair of someone
I once knew, I loop them round
the shoulders of this kitchen chair

so, by myself, I can untease
them, wind them into balls,
plot a chunky polo-neck for him
to keep out winds that freeze

when he is roughing quaysides
easing ships from port. My fingers
have by now an understanding of
his winds and tides.

Cable-stitch of course. Out there
he's casting off – unhitching ropes –
as I cast on, knitting something
else for him to wear.

Out of love or loneliness or gall?
All seem precariously true.
Needles click away the seconds, my hands,
jabbing, shadow-box upon the wall.

OUT THERE

Out there, he said,
meaning the lashed dark,
gale-driven seas, flung prow, tumbling decks,
swaggering deck-hand manliness.

Out there, he said,
meaning bays they rode
at anchor in, sauciness, hazardous
drunken pleasurings, distant rooms.

Out there, he said,
meaning the fisted street,
concrete pavements, back-biting swank,
bleak politics, the what-we-have-to-settle-for.

Out there, he said,
meaning blustery docks, companionship with gulls,
lumbering cranes, ropes stiff as girders,
the where-we-get-the-money-from;

meaning blown dust, dissolution,
scurrying atoms, dispersing universe,
the where-we-all-get-to-in-the-end.

IN HERE

In here, she said,

meaning
four staring walls,

unspeakable liquids,
barely understood,
obdurately governing her,

meaning
an attic space
of stacked-up memories and hurt.

In here, she said,

meaning
words locked
in a diary never penned,
in letters never sent,

a drawer of kitchen knives
rusting away,

a playground of devils,
bullying nerves.

In here, she said finally,

meaning
a black-hearted tumour
squared-up-to, desolately defied.

FOUND AMONG THE EFFECTS

for Maureen

a sheet wrenched
from an old exercise book,
an earnest before-bed
pencilled *thank-you-for-*
the-Easter-egg,

an innocence of words...
so happy I could shout
whoopee...

in a hand
crassly failing
to match the courtly strokes
and roundnesses
of Teacher's
blackboard copperplate –

hard evidence
of a forgotten me
over fifty years ago
when I was Mattie,
and couldn't spell:

Mam said she will
hard boil it
and keep it as
a silvenear

emphatic with kisses,
forty-six
to match the year,

kept
(love in a shoe-box)
all this while...

HER GRANDDAUGHTER

Remember how she strained to keep herself alive,
cranked up in bed in that distempered hospital,
anxious for us to fetch the baby in to her;

how she held her, whispered 'take good care of her',
handing the baby back; and how that night we understood
the meaning of the blood-racket in her throat, how we

would carry home the will to keep alive whatever
happened between them, a dying woman, sleeping child,
whatever urgent interchange of love there'd been.

UNEXPECTED LEGACY

A 'little something' to remember him by:
a solicitor's cheque, its *please-acknowledge-sign-below*,
come with junk-mail, out of the blue of the post.

Late to the family, an unplanned uncle,
with no sense of ships, our way with bales of cotton,
sacks of sugar, shipped-out cars and chemicals,
the creosote-smell of ropes our men brought home,

a slap-happy Mr Polly, he brought the commerce-smell
of high-street furnishers: tape-measures, bills for curtains,
Wilton carpets, lino, leatherette settees.

Set hard for spinsterhood, Ruby kept her Sunday afternoons
for tea-and-biscuit talk of A-level grades (*our Maureen*'s future),
in a parlour life of Mills and Boon, with telly nights:
of Corrie, Minstrel Shows, upholstered Doonicans.

Daft-lad on a motor-bike, he whizzed her off
to countrysides – the Peak, the mint-cake Lakes,
the Trough of Bowland – togged in leathers, goggles,
as if they fled a gas-attack. Played smoochy
dance-band trumpet too. What wouldn't I
have given to hear him swank his way through
Try a Little Tenderness, I Get Along Without You Very Well!
But then he had the accident that crooked his body,
made him twitch, ruined his puff and fingering...though
never his Jack-the-lad Scouse cockiness.

When Ruby died, I watched him at the crematorium
carted down the aisle like some hapless wino
in a hospital A & E, unwashed, unshaven, all
his broken love on show.

Something to remember him by? Better the brick-
by-careful-brick construction of a late-in-life happiness,
the straightforwardness and sureness of his love.

Unexpected uncle, I tell you now, speaking up too late,
I'd have gladly swapped the solicitor's cheque
for your Eddie Calvert trumpet...and something of your lip.

A LAST PHOTOGRAPH OF MY FATHER

a one-time
ocean-going man
looking out to sea,
leaning wistfully
on a Welsh town's
municipal seaside rails,
dabbed for the summer
a lime-green gloss.

There are glowering
purple mountains
to his right.

He's on
his second honeymoon,
a second wife,
one eye scrunched up,
behind the lens;

he is as proper as ever,
in suit and tie,
(this is earnest 'going-out')
mac obligatory over one arm;

even so
a weather-eye is telling him
those greyish clouds
now sneaking in
are ready to do
unsettling things.

He is staring out
(as if there's need to expiate)
at half-a-lifetime of bad faith.

The sea is saying
nothing back to him;
tide gravely sliding away,
shipping out those breezy ghosts
he'd like to parley with and who

already know how soon, how far inland,
his ashes will be blown.

EXPLAINING THINGS

The last treason
is to want a reason.
Gael Turnbull

Those days it was enough
to say *she suffers with her nerves.*
There was even something
aristocratic about it – the delicacy
of wine-glass stems, chantilly lace.
They'd say *She is a lady is your mum,*
admire the way she always had
of *keeping to herself.*

Reasons come with hindsight:
a disapproved-of marriage, my 'difficult birth',
him away at sea, the screaming Blitz,
kinks in the spirals of the genes.

But reason won't explain
the swept-up-out-of-nowhere dread that kills
a street stone dead, that drills in deep
the present tense of your any-moment death.

My mother half-lived a half-sized life;
not understanding, did what she bravely could.

Sometimes you'd catch her murmuring
You know what Thought did! He followed
a muck-cart, thought it was a wedding.

TALKING WITH A DEAD MAN

i.m. Tony Mills

What did you want?
To watch your life come hurtling back,
man gasping, clutching at rocks,
a fast-frame, last-ditch buying back?

Was it a calling-in of debts from those
whose lives made play with yours,
on which you left some shadowy print,
the need to know you'd lived
and lived to some effect?

You can't answer, can't complain
how just/unjust what I'm implying is:
perhaps that's why you had to get in first
with last goodbyes.

Talking with the dead's a glib pretence
that we can put things right some way.
You're gone nowhere and that's a place
perplexes with its blankness; there's no
reporting back from there. So why haul
back through mirrors this let's-pretend,
dig deep in the pocket for words to spend
kidding ourselves we're buying time?

So when, after a day's grim hesitation,
I acted at last on a friend's passed-on request
to phone, things were already critical,
your kidneys already cinders, your voice not just
two hundred miles away
but three-quarters down the road to somewhere else.

And when it came to saying goodbye
it sounded like what poets strive for,
words used absolutely, that can't be got rid of,
that enter space, hang about.

STOPS ALONG THE WAY

for John Farrell

The first day of the second Iraqi war, I'm on the Northern Line,
rattling out through Liverpool and Bootle, towards the
    sand-duned shores
of Formby, Freshfield, the long flatness of the Lancashire Plain.

Elderly people crowd the carriage with their rucksacks,
    lunch-packs, bonhomie,
for their mid-week hike, josh each other above the clamour of
    the rails,
prattling of rambles, hedgerows, lanes, and timbered pubs, as if
only the past's worth visiting, nothing's happening anywhere
    else.

This journey does the same to me, compels me into history.

Once through the grumbling tunnel under shopping-centre
    Liverpool,
light lunges back with dull-as-pewter glimpses of the river,
glum Victorian warehouses, gull-infested docks where my father
    worked
and I stuck out vacation jobs among outlandish hard-knock
    men...
Now it's rare to find a funnel, catch the movement of a crane.

Then birthplace Bootle, with its sooty grim town hall,
where up the flagpole we six-formers ran a pair of bloomers
    once
and where I heard classical music for the first time live
    ...Dvorak's brave
New World, under the baton of a white-haired Reginald Jacques.

There's the *Wyndham* Joe Ellis drank at lunchtime in
before he'd face another class like ours....and the spooky
    shopping centre
called The Strand, where Jamie Bulger was coaxed away.

14

Next Seaforth Sands, nearest stop to our old house in bombed-
    out
Bulwer Street; another half-forgotten war, and the redbrick
    workhouse walls
of Gray Street Junior School where poetry began with *Banks and
    Braes*;
and then the Cinder Path to the Coliseum picture-house through
    which
we scuffed our way to bang-bang Hollywood; and there's that
    blue-brick bridge
where murder-legend scared our childhoods stiff.

And now posher Crosby in which I trained to be a pharmacist
before I got the call, the message of 'good books.'

At length the dunes, the svelte golf-courses of the middle-class I
    once despised.

The elderly are on their feet – their stop at last – swinging
    back-packs up,
off to invade the country, occupy and liberate territory of the
    mind.

A day-out couple opposite remain. She points to daffodils
in garden-backs, he nodding quietly, confirming everything she
    says...
as if days are luxuries they have agreed to share.

Next stop mine. It is the first day of another war and I am
    visiting a friend
to share music with: the explosive sadness of Tchaikovsky,
    Holst's *Mars*
the relentless *Bringer of War*, *Venus the* benighted *Bringer of
    Peace.*

YOUNG LOVE ON THE TRAIN

I

They are so confident, so together. Sharing
an apple so deeply red you'd think
a wicked-witch stepdame had presented it.
They nibble reverently, in turns, certain
there's no evil. Now she is scrutinising his hands,
length of fingers, condition of his cuticles,
and searching not his eyes but mouth, as lovers will,
for confirmation she knows there's really
no occasion for...

It's a game. She understands the rules enough
to make this play of publicly ignoring them.
She knows I'm looking, tucks her head, as if
behaving normally, into his shoulder. A rebuke.
I am required to look away, out of the window:
at houses, hedges, cattle, fences, fields, hurtling past.

II

I want to overstate with 'lordly'
for he is almost that.

If I could slowmotion
his gestures, movements,

they would seem
balletic, sculpting certainties.

See how, almost indifferent,
he lets her take his hand

and play his fingers
like an instrument,

how unfussed he is each time
she tenders the apple to his mouth,

how trusting his shoulder is
when, taunting my stare,

she snuggles in to him.

All down the line, she's the one
making the moves.

Watching her, wondering what next
she'll do, I'm envious of

the knowledge he seems master of,
his unassailable aplomb.

A PACKAGE TO THE WRONG ADDRESS.

No postcode, and not our name,
from Plymouth where we know
no-one. I browsed the internet
for same-name roads, found one
twelve miles from here,
indiscreetly opened up to see
perhaps who'd posted it.

Photographs from a wedding,
middle-aged men severe in suits,
women grand in frothy hats,
a note, with no address, for *Joan*
from *Thelma* expressing hope
the journey back was not
too tedious Strangers' lives
and their engrossing intimacies.

I phoned a friend whose directory helped.
The name (misspelt) was near enough,
an address confirmed. I got the number, rang.

Someone was surprised to hear my voice. I asked
the postcode, sent the package on.

Images remain. Which one is Thelma,
who is Joan, buffeting for place
on church door steps? Who is whose husband?
Why do they look austere instead of pleased?
What young man picked up the phone?
Joan's son? Who married whom?
Why don't they leave me alone?

CICADAS

I'd like to get a word in edgeways,
here on the balcony beside
this feathery tamarisk
ablaze with sound.

I'd like to raise my glass of ouzo,
milky as semen, high
in the late afternoon, to you
and procreation.

That's all you sing of, you
and your jazzy legs! And yet
to catch you at it needs
a laser eye. Yes, there,

like a tiny flake of bark,
one of invisible thousands
filling branches
with high voltage noise!

Hard to believe you don't migrate
from tree to tree. Our tamarisk's
become an abrupt silence
and in the pistachio orchard over the way

another tree is all a-fizz.
Now suddenly you're back:
every single one of you
switched – presto – on again.

THE DAY WE SAW DOLPHINS

for John Lucas

persuaded me some god
should be acknowledged.

How else explain
the synchronicity

of giving each other
the same gift? Hadn't you said

how rarely dolphins swam
around the island now,

regretting what I'd miss,
might never share? Then

suddenly Look! I yelled,

out in the shimmering bay,
five, yes, five broad backs

sewing the turquoise sea
to a dusky purple sky.

How else describe the joy I felt,
the joy I saw in you,

your wished-for possibility,
my discovering it?

CALLERS

They ring the bell, two of them,
bringing their insistent news.

The black guy's turn...
stubbly beard, grandfatherly eyes,
West Indian smile...his cue
to start us off with talk about
the 'terrible state of things'.
He wonders (a ploy to coax me
into acquiescence) how God
'can allow such wickedness
in the world today.'

I don't invite them in
(indoors there are enough
injustices to exercise);
and I resist declaring I'm
a Metaphysical Marxist,
an Independent Methodist,
or telling them how Zen
once helped unglue my mind.

Instead I think of Blake's
Nobodaddy, God of Vengeance,
Lord of Thou-Shalt-Not
and reply 'We should ban
capital-G God from the universe.'
.
The bright evangelical light
goes out of their eyes at my apostasy.

'But what about loving your neighbour?'

Again I think of Blake's other God
of Mercy, Pity, Peace and Love.

'You don't need,' I insist, 'a bad old deity
for that...and in any case not all neighbours
deserve one's love. Goodbye.'

THE MAN WHO LOVES BARGAINS

for John Ireland

They know him in the charity shops,
a discerning rummager
through compact discs,
a sideways scanner of spines of books
on Art, Music, First World War.

It's Mr Ireland again!
Good morning, Mr Ireland!

There's not a library sale,
flea-market stall, bargain basement,
Barnados, Oxfam, Marie Curie, Christian Aid
he doesn't know about.

He's rescuing spurned, once-valued things;
making a brave but ineffectual critique
of the throw-away society;
affirming kinship with a great artistic past;
aspiring to ideals of excellence;
donating a senior citizen's mite;

above all, it says he's long been on
a pilgrimage of grace
to tucked-away places where God's
been gathering dust.

Consider his house,
stacked like a Pharaoh's pyramid.
What it says is, 'God,
I have brought together these movables
to offer up as worship. I would like them
to sustain me in eternity, to represent
the *me* I have been trying to become;

I would be privileged to shake hands
with their makers
for fashioning whatever I have of soul.'

22

KIND OF BLUE

If you're going to heaven, might as well
go first-class all the way.
                    CD sleeve-note

The music had gotten thick, Miles croaked,
forehead shiny with sweat. He wanted
melodic rather than harmonic variation...
wanted *infinite possibilities.* And he got them,
sucked them in and blew them out,
such streams of melody, all that mattered
was listening to the music explore itself.

It must have been made in heaven,
Jimmy Cobb, his drummer, grinned.

OLD HANDS

(portrait of a jazz pianist at 80)

They say jazz is a country of the old,
of left-over men, guys with grizzled beards,
plaits or ponytails, out-of-date dudes
with drawled allusions to the hoary
good old days of hip and swing and cool,
cats in awe of cats they learnt from,
the real McCoys that went before.

This piano-man for one looks out of sync,
grey head nodding, answering slow, but still
chipper with irony, indulging
his pushy TV questioner. Then wanting
to rattle keys again, saying 'Let me illustrate...'

So now take two hands in close-up. Not backward
in coming forward. Ten fingers, charged with cunning,
scampering like king crabs, racing the tide.

ONLY A THIMBLEFUL

for Julie London

A thimbleful of a voice, you called it,
lips brushing the microphone
as you began, shimmeringly, to sing.

We slipped into a dream of whispers
meant only for us. A molten mezzo
with a sixty-cigarettes-a-day come-hither voice,

who cried us rivers, through moonless nights,
beneath blue moons. And too good to be true,
you were a face in the misty light,

our Laura of the misty voice who whispered
what we could expect of love: husky words
kept handy, like just-in-case condoms
in inside pockets, sexual IOUs.

BANKS OF GREEN WILLOW

i.m. the composer, George Butterworth,
killed 5th August, 1915

I would like,
before it was too late,
to have got down there,
into the smashed fields of Pozières,

have stood upright in no-man's-land,
arms outstretched like the crucified one
and shouted 'halt!';

and supposing by some miracle
it worked, I would,
in the perplexed silence into which
birds suddenly returned,
have sought out
George Butterworth;

and, arm around
his muddied shoulders, limped
him out of the shallow trench
bearing his name,
with its splashed blood and brains,
into his denied future;

brought him back
to the damaged landscapes of sweet home,
and, in the promise of healing symphonies,
sat him down with paper, pens...

SHAKESPEARE'S SONNETS

Who exactly's on the other side? Who's
The second-person-singular, the one
The fretful poet's always talking to,
Guaranteeing eternal life? What swan-
Feathered sonnets are rhyming dustily
Somewhere on the lost side of the equation?
Would they tell why the poet's earnestly
Rebutting what clearly's accusation?
O call not me to justify the wrong,
O never say that I was false of heart,
by *naming thy name blesses... ill report?*
Who *from the for-lorne* must *his visage hide*
In the silvered glass's Stygian other side?

LA DAME AUX CAMÉLIAS

Between boudoir and board, the theatre is
our Parisian *beau monde's* most egregious craze,
a shop-window for strumpets, and, right at the heart,

Marie Duplessis flaunting herself abroad
every scented evening, dazzling all
with the fanfaronade of her flouncing gowns:

all those Dukes and propertied gallants vying to fork out
lavish sums for favours – each one hungry for
more than gymnastic mummery of common whores

with voluptuous figures but lacking all finesse.
Wasn't she once a laundry girl with sour
scrubbing-board hands, a back-street dressmaking nobody?

Like other *papillons* of that glimmer-world
of *demi-reps*, someone making good, seductive,
glitzy, literate, a charming conversationalist, at ease

in the best society, but, *hélas*, sentenced terminally,
a pale consumptive heroine strolling gaily
into tragic opera on the nonchalant arm of a rich grandee.

AND ONCE AT LUMB BANK

for Anne Stevenson

"What comes from the heart goes to the heart."
                                        Coleridge

In the theatre there's always that desire
not to break the silence following a great performance,
even with applause;
                        the same sometimes with music
when you're so attentive you become 'the music
while the music lasts.'

The first time I listened to Schubert's String Quintet,
and later the Bruckner Ninth, I went out each time
into a stunned unspeaking night to walk an hour.

And again, one blustery winter's evening
in a candle-flickering King's Chapel, that Russian
Orthodox Choir, the profoundest of basses
deepening the gloom beyond the rood screen
long into the silence afterwards.

It happens rarely with poetry, when reading out
should make discussion after prodigal, that is
when rhythms, nuances, music, voice go to the heart,
to 'all one's ears alive'...and you are in
a 'gentle, auditory,/slow hallucination'

You read out Bishop's *Moose* and had us bumping along ...
'on red gravelly roads,/down rows of sugar maples,/past
clapboard farmhouses/and neat, clapboard churches,/bleached,
ridged as clamshells,/past twin silver birches,/through late
afternoon'...cocking ears for fellow-passenger chit-chat,
and nodding, yes, 'Life's like that'...each one of us alive
with the 'sweet/sensation of joy' when the moose
halted the chugging westward bus....

Then when the bus
crunched on, we were all 'craning backwards',
squinnying at something dwindling 'on the moon-
lit macadam', our nostrils spiked with the 'dim/smell of moose,
an acrid/smell of gasoline.'

At once the world was 'minute and vast and clear'.

We had become the poem.

II

NOVEMBER SONG

an uncompleted sequence

The days dwindle down...
Maxwell Anderson & Kurt Weill

Let us have winter loving that the heart
May be in peace and ready to partake
Of the slow pleasure spring would wish to hurry
Or that in summer harshly would awake,
And let us fall apart, O gladly weary,
The white skin shaken like a white snowflake.
Elizabeth Jennings

In the event
the event is sacrificed
to a fiction of its having happened.
Anne Stevenson

Here's a maze trod indeed
Through forthrights and meanders.
The Tempest

Prelude

Under the poem's branches two people
Walk and even the words are shy.
                W. S. Graham

Make sense of her. Probe the nerves
to find the woman curled there foetus-like
within the pith of me,

Hard for her to live with peace,
she who skipped in blood and played
on blitz-smashed masonry.

Fastness in the tissues of my love
cannot preclude unbidden trepidations
and twitching in her dreams.

Try then to make sense of her
within/beyond the consternations of my self,

Imagine her moving through water,
uncoiling the braids of her hair,
myself the water holding her,

think her the vulnerable and uncertain pulse

of possible poems.

Strange Meeting

Go back to our beginnings,
forty years:

you a foreign red-haired cover-girl,
bare shoulders, deep resentful eyes,
glossy high heels stabbing at
the gravel of the drive, clacking
up the steps, in my direction,
a technicolour girl, come to class
to master phrasal verbs and me,
a beautiful vagueness I need somehow
to focus and to clarify.
Later, after my Optional
Evening Lecture you walk towards me
like a dare and ask to borrow notes,
my 'Poets of the First World War'.

It was Christmas in no-man's land,
a euphoria of *hey johnnie let's shake hands,
sing songs, knock back a few, play games,*

the allure of consonantal rhyme.

Ich Bin Ein Berliner

There I was in Berlin, a few weeks married,
mucking about on a bed in your mother's flat,
sock on head, another mimicking a beard,
dangly tulip in one hand, and you calling me
your *garten zwerg*.
                    Your mother had announced
'Tonight we will all become a hot-water bottle!' puzzled why
we'd laughed…and me still wondering why, suspicious
of my nose, she'd whispered 'Is your man a Jew?'

I didn't think then that I might be in hostile territory,
the site of curdled memories, screeching bombs,
advancing tanks and foreign men, focus of everything
that had gone wrong for you. I know it now. Then I was
wide-eyed, a tourist, being shown where Kennedy had stood
to say 'I am a doughnut', then a dividing wall, barbed wire,
soldiers with guns, binoculars trained on me.

Note: in German the verb 'bekommen' means to get, obtain; 'garten
zwerg' is a garden gnome, and a Berliner a kind of doughnut.

Pique Dame

- Tchaikovsky on DVD

All operas are long, the singers too old,
too plump for what is meant. Matronly nymphs
who trip and flounce and lovelorn barrel-chested swains
who strut and fret their little hours of fame away.

You make allowances. Death normally gets
the better of them, sorts things out.

You and I, love, remember differently. Tonight
the anguished tenor's sweating his deep
Slavic soul out has you picking on
and chuckling over Russian words,
phrases from a schoolgirl time long before me,
and his barge-booted clumping makes you think
of stages you – Cordelia, Abigail – once bustled on.

I've homed in on the soprano, her *vivace*
willingness to fall; finding myself in thrall
to a memory of the first time you walked
steadily naked towards me, a stark
inverted triangle of dark hair, dramatic, meant.

Tongues

A woman is a foreign land,
Of which, though there he settle young,
A man will ne'er quite understand
The customs, politics, and tongue.
                    Coventry Patmore

In my case, not much to speak of:
enough French for shunting words –
Molière's, Lamartine's – across a page;
enough Latin to conjugate and pass
examinations with, Caesar's footslogging
cohorts, Cicero at sixty, 'with no diminution to
his ardent feelings or his intellect…'

Let's drink to that. And also to
your old Berlin *gymnasium* English
which travelled further, brought you here.

You never intended it but love grabbed you
in a sticky language web.
(Do we measure love by what we sacrifice?)

I don't much know what it's like to act
to a script in a tongue that's not my own.
'How's your German?' people ask.
'She's fine,' I answer, ashamed of how
I twice gave up, afraid of syntax,
Hitler words that bite. Like when
my cackhanded feet once fled
a ballroom dancing class, fearful of becoming
politically someone else.

What does it say of me? That I don't love enough
to conjugate and pass? And what of you when you
began dreaming in English, walking about
with somebody else's tongue in your head?

In the Wings

Once you were able to focus
so thoroughly
on being someone else
that, during one
performance of a play,
a safety pin
jabbed in your side
till some time after
the moment of your walking off.
Only then you felt the pain
of being backstage you again.

I can remember once
watching from the wings,
overhearing a different you
elegantly speaking classical verse
in a painted grove.

You belonged
to Dis's plaster columns,
canvas clouds,

and when you came
towards me
in a swish
of borrowed silks

I could not match
your radiance,
the spotlight spell
which you were under still.

I was Orpheus
come to take you back.

You were,
for all the world,
Eurydice.

Red Shoes

We watch the film, its verve,
those eccentrically
well-spoken words,
the poignant classic choice
of love or art,

Moira Shearer's hair
exactly yours,
the red you flaunted
when you posed
for German glamour mags
and we first met,

you in recoil from tackiness,
the pretensions and the sleaze
of film and television work,
come to Cambridge
to – how do you say ? –
'brush my English up',

me your teacher telling how
to pronounce your words
like the characters
in early English films like this.

It was meant to be temporary.

But here we are
all these years later, choices made
for better, for worse,
watching idealised images
of our younger selves,
prancing too earnestly on DVD,
our hair now grey
as weathered straggles of wool
snatched at by barbed wire.

Reported Missing

I'd go if 1 could. I'd take a thousand pounds
like our friend Jan who just tramped off
to Tibet to find out more about death. I'd buy
a sensible anorak, back-pack, and go,
leave tomorrow, except you need to keep me here;

not just because I'd cock up your birthday,
the grandchildren coming, the cake, but because
you hardly trust yourself enough to think
that I'd come back. And yet I'd like to go
on some forlorn adventure soon... let's say

to trace (there is the slimmest chance he's still
alive) the father who fifty years ago marched out
on you, who, under orders, (weren't they all?)
trudged into Russia through unimaginable snows.
His grey old photograph (when people thought

photography was theft and always looked afraid)
declares a bookish horn-rimmed man
whose unpreparedness is plain. I like to think
he dragged his rifle wearily into that blizzarding East.
'Reported Missing' is where I'd start.

I'd bring him back if it meant healing you
of half a life's distrust. Maybe he did slink off
into a wood, and over mountains, made it back
in time to see the rubble of Berlin; perhaps
like my father, home from sea, among the bricks

of our bombed street, he shrugged and thought
he'd come too late. I can't pretend it isn't hazardous.
Telly daily pounds buildings into rockeries,
borders shift, men with rifles dodge
round pockmarked walls.

You can count on crossfire, mortar shells, mines,
the old historical certainties. 1 think it would be
worth it. But then that's me talking. Tomorrow's
your birthday, time and the need to brave it out again.

Taurus and Gemini

For just one month
straddling May and June
we share the same age, love,
after which you charge ahead,
aiming next for that three-score-and-ten
everyone assures us we'll survive.

I'm not competitive. I've no immediate wish
to catch you up. Nor am I jealous.
I'll go on waiting for those odd in-common weeks
to come just when and as we know they will.

Casablanca

Those eyes of deep, soft, lucent hue –
Eyes too expressive to be blue,
Too lovely to be grey –
                    Matthew Arnold

We are revisiting another old movie. Contentions
in black-and-white. Nazis taking Paris,
people scurrying South. Lovers making promises
we know they cannot keep. Everything going up in smoke.

He waits at the rain-drenched station. She doesn't come,
the girl he loves and now must learn to live without. The same
old story. Choice of love or duty, do or die. He'll later realise.
Now he feels betrayed. Lights one more sardonic fag, moves on.

Yet can't forget her eyes and their soft-focus urgency.
Nor that song that lingers in them like a steadfast gleam.
Their theme-song. He tries to blank it out. That is until
ineluctably they meet again. Then *Play it, Sam!*

Now thinking of us, love: here's looking at you and me! both
survived. You clambering out of a Berlin cellar clutching dolls;
me a Bootle air-raid shelter's huddling dark. We were lucky.
Met. Made promises we mostly managed to keep.

Star Gazing

For nights I have been watching Mars
climb the window, scale the gap between
fraying curtains, maintain a slow
and sure trajectory that rises out of Cheshire
and heads for splashdown in the Irish Sea;
watched it glide above television's fiddle-faddle
like something intended, an eye kept on things.

Each night on cue it undertakes an as-if-
scripted progress over the roofs
of Fords, Eli Lilly, St Andrew's Church.
And now into mid-September,
hustled down the Mersey by puny rockets,
remains steadfast and unfazed. Some nights,
muffled by cloud, it journeys on behind
a seamless blackness, sure as love.
God knows, we need something to rely on:
the house is a jangle of nerves, a desperate
clutter of debris, emotional dross. More winds
blow inside than out. Malicious ghosts
treat it as a home from home. It needs
slowmotioning, a star to hitch its good-will to.

Nervous Disposition

...phobic horror is a baffling of expectation;
there is nothing but paralysis or flight.
                    Adam Phillips

Woozy from waking, I shuffle down
to breakfast, do the morning check
for emails, find a note in your
big girlie hand, waiting for me on the desk.

Too easy to think and say this is
unfair and cowardly, puts the squeeze
on me, you ruthless to have me
stay indoors again, not rock the boat.

No haircut again today.

What choice is there? Unless I want
to let you down. No, I need to be at hand
in case, in case...

                    And so to fill the day again:
crosswords, novels, other people's poetry,
looking forward to whatever post, the evening's soap,
wine that turns to acid in my craw,

maybe write nervy and self-justifying things like these.

An Autumn Rose

So much, I know, depends on me.

Let's be positive, you say.
Not always easy when, deprived of choice,
the ability to come and go at will,
I stiffen into glum resentment like a child
kept in and punishing the world with sulks.
When I try it works,
seems such a simple thing to do.

This morning I discover on my desk a rose
fetched from the garden, an October rose,
and by its side a shy lover's letter shaming me,
thanking me for being kind.

Tending

After years of promises, I managed
to get round to it this time, as one might with
a second honeymoon, an eternity ring,
re-papering a room: I daubed both front
and back with showy annuals, cheap, ground-
hugging plants to hide the soil.

Petunias did best, keeping a vulgar riot up
for months, flashy fairground sassiness beyond
first frost and rot of leaves. The roses had
been manicured, blasé far too long, an outré
aristocracy with keep-your-distance thorns.

Tiddly-pom and the thrill of the circus, love!

Enough grounds here for doing it all again.

Sinfonia

It's secrets make us sick. Hildegard von Bingen kept
God's voice all to herself till late in life,
always needing permission, an Affirmation,
to write her woman's worth of wisdom down.

Denial made her ill. And when at last the Church
did give her leave to be herself, to write her visions down,
no longer torpid with fear, she felt the grasp of fullness.

Her music could proclaim a union of soul and body.
What she wanted to say was the world is indivisible,
rejoices in veriditas, you learn to trust your leaping into God.

The Courage of Tenderness

So much to recover from,
undo, unlearn,
so many years' defence
against what-if...

suddenly there's hope
of rejoicing
in being vulnerable again,

wanting
to put the present right,
make our bit
of future tolerable,

get back to something,

the way things used to be,

uncertain what they were

but desperate to try.

Second Thoughts

One click
and yesterday's
booed-off comma
comes coolly walking on again;
another
and a whole
cashiered paragraph
files back in:
deftly I redeem
discarded adjectives,
recover verbs,
repent, make good.

If Macbeth had written
his bloody narrative
and had been able to undo
what had been done,
he would have been
less grimly visceral.
A mouse
unkills a king,
deletes a ghost.
All to do with
memory, ordering things
on screen.

Real-life days
(Macbeth was right)
can't be re-lived
nor deeds undone,
and only a fraction's
ever returned
of what we say
we will take back
and never do
or say again.

What if we could
click back
to where we saved
yesterday's
good intentions,
cut and paste – and justify –
into today?

Clearing Out

is something I sometimes threaten, dream of more and more,
clambering out and tramping shell-shocked back
past glumly marshalled others moving up the line,

gone forever-fishing, tranced by ripples, leaving behind
this over-lived-in house which we've re-roofed, repainted,
double-glazed, which never quite shrugs off its thought

of others gone before, their hedges, built-in wardrobes,
their square-cut lawns that keep me dutiful. Mortgage paid,
six years of pension, and still our old dynamic yanks me back:

my if-only's, your yes-but's alive enough to neuter choice.
Clearing out today's rhetorical again, symbolic shuffling off,
before plumbers arrive to unbolt, rip out, replace the boiler,

so we become more economical with heat. Chucking out
from this one small corner, I'm at least creating gangway, room,
ruthless in the way that you are holding on to things. And

it makes you edgy, this not honouring your kind of
    remembering.
When you quote time and place you know of things exact to
    wind
or wound me with; not *when* but *where* is where I'm good:

streets, roads, bookshops, pubs. You won't relinquish hold.
Your just-in-case with screwtops, coffee jars, cartons, envelopes,
plastic bags, and me, is you surviving a war you hardly think is
    over.

The outhouse clutter's binbagged now. But I can't be sure you
    won't
go rooting catlike, rummaging in the dark, clawing back
    mildewed
curtains, sandals without buckles, carpet offcuts coughing dust,
handbags without handles, to coddle in some other hideyhole.

That Old Feeling

Elgar, Famous Grouse, and a summer night
with nothing much in mind. Except to flirt
with clichés. O.K., clichés are only truth
with some immediacy rubbed off.
Memory's loitering with intent of something
sensuous; love wanting to feel itself again.
Recapture/rapture if I were
in rhyming Ella or Sinatra mood.

I'm hoping for a particular night
over forty years ago. Simon loping round to that
old murky Cambridge flat of ours and you
beautiful in pregnancy. He was expecting too:
First Novel any day – go-ahead, anxious,
dead ringer for Eliot at Harvard in 1906.

I've doubts of his remembering this. We didn't
keep in touch. But you remembered: the talk,
the jokes, and how he said
you hardly looked...
                    That night you woke me up
we had no coppers for the phone,
we packed some things and walked a mile
to Mill Road Hospital. The stars were beautiful.

In Deep

Keeping my head down, I hear your voice,
but not the words you speak,
bouncing from blue-glazed tiles.

It's not so much that I'm not listening.
Just not hearing. In deep. Not up to but over
my ears, searching the bottom for quietness

and trying to keep steady, alternating lengths
of breaststroke, crawl. I have two
mosaic dolphins down here to contemplate,

their unforced smiles, the way they have,
like saucy lovers, of touching one another.
It's not that I don't realise

we are, and have for long, been in
this together. Goggles off and heavier each step,
I wade out to shower, asking what you said.

Twin Beds in Venice

Judging from the pictures,
Hell looks the more
interesting place.
                    Japanese Senryū

I'm shaken by my friend's account of how
in sleep I struggle with 'demons' half the night,
rev to climaxes that seem to want
to burst me out of it but rarely do. It's as if

I've trudged across the Bridge of Sighs,
with one last glimpse of the hazed lagoon,
to slink and slump into the Doge's dungeons, there
thrash about and whimper like the damned

in those fresco-Hells that we've been looking at
all week. I'd naively thought of sleep as decorous,
that what went on in dreams fussed only the mind.
Now it's indecent, a betrayal of something intimate

by a self I do not, and can never, really know.
Yet if I did (albeit he's no mate of mine, I can
imagine him a Trickster with Punchinello nose,
waggish jaw, hinting at secrets, a misdirected life),

would he be someone reading palms, dictating poems;
would I cadge or nick his mask and go to Hell
in Venice with that bad and dangerous man
who aptly named the Bridge?

Abroad Again Without You

(a postcard)

This time playing the boulevardier in Cannes,
observing how people make their bodies move:
old biddies prancing with pink-bowed pooches in their arms,
safari men shuffling about in sandals, shorts, lenses dangling,
chic floozies in shades catwalking through the sun's applause.

What confidence money and sunlight afford!

Behind me, the cannonball clunk of men at boules
and immigrant nobodies, bundles of rags, inert on benches
under shadowing palms; and beyond, a blue Mediterranean
hazing into Africa, a hot rich-man's sun skimming the harbour's
white-enamel yachts all going nowhere with bikini'd women
busily waving hoses and red-bellied men slouching on deck.

The heat refuses to let me get used to myself, a self all
        too aware
of things not shared, money leeching away
in a pampered pampering other-world.

Voices from an Island

Prospero.　*How now? Moody?*
　　　　　What is't thou canst demand?
Ariel.　　*My liberty.*

i *Ariel Remembers Sycorax*

With her I thought I had some choice,
at least an option to refuse. She made me
pay for my dissent: confined me like
a gnat in amber all those years.

Was I meant to groan perpetually?
What choice when saying no
means every twist and turn
jags you with splinters, wood or ice?

He's as bad, this conjuror I serve.
'It was mine art,' he says, 'that let thee out.'

What for? To serve his turn and be beholden,
do his tricks for him, else receive
the old treatment, crammed into
the innards of an oak like stuffing in a goose?

Sleep-deprivation is the thing. He's good, like her,
at midnight cramps. Just a game of chess to him:
corner the king, see off the knights.
Two days I'm promised. Do I trust him?
What will I do with my freedom, what will it do with me?

ii *Prospero's Thinking*

If things don't work out

I always have my treasury of books,
their various infinite musics.

Ducal library, cave piled high
makes little difference.

My job's to make the narratives come clean,
simply getting timings right,

though I must confess
I often have bad dreams.

iii *Sycorax Appears in a Dream*

Impossible for you to imagine me
anywhere else but cramped up in
the syllables of others,
unvilified, without a name that sounds
like boots stamping on cockroaches;

impossible to picture a non-witch
sans bastard, sans misshapen whelp,
any kind of redress. Long dead
before curtain-up, unable to enter left or right,
not free to speak up for myself.

But what a soliloquist I'd make!

No matter! For the moment let me say
we all find our own ways of surviving –
some secret, magical, all ultimately
practical – of learning how to live,
how to fend off death.

iv *Caliban Thinks About Freedom*

What's freedom to the dispossessed? Words.
Who taught me words. Him. Why?

To make a fiction of me. Whose story? His.
Freedom? Swapping servitudes more like.

Why did he show me beautiful things? Especially her.
Reason? Make me see the brute in me. Now

I no longer seek my features in a pool or listen to
my voice among the whispering ferns.

Who's going to free me from the dreams I have,
this tingle of music always in my ears?

v *What Miranda Thinks*

Can't wait to get out of the place
now I know a whole new world's out there.

Pictures in my father's books have come to life,
they talk, they breathe, they have desires too.

Already I've changed eyes with the best of them
that speak my language. Can't wait

to leave this penitential place, go with them
out of my father's history into something of my own.

vi *Ferdinand Butts In*

My royal father's fathoms deep among the corals,
scuttling crabs. If I may, I'd like a word.

First there's him. Making me fetch and carry...
but then there's thought of her. Worth giving up

some freedom for. Play a waiting game, risk a bit
of harmless cheating. Worth trying to be virtuous for.

vii *Stephano Passes the Bottle*

Take comfort in this. Purge your mind
with pleasant fumes of wine.
Fill up your veins. Don't mind me.
Empty your head Get beyond singing.

Feel free.

Soon enough dead.

viii *Good Old Gonzalo*

Old man who needs sometimes to dream of better things.
Possible places. More gentle, kind. Country to retire to,
be wise, respected in. Where everything has care for others
and itself. Without sovereignty. A commonwealth.

What am I doing here on this ungovernable isle?
Weathering silences, the grief when words go wrong,
abuse of malcontents, inexplicable mood swings of the sea.
And of course simply trying to make the best of it.

Reply to Someone Who Got Things Badly Wrong

Now you draw away, and all you've said, all you've done,
is long gone, words in the wind, clouds the sky lets go.
But if you forget, the gods, remember, good faith, remember,
will make you repent, at length, for all harm rendered.

Catullus trans. Josephine Balmer

I

Of course friends find it hard;
most try to understand and largely do,
at least they sympathise. But you,
who'd have thought that, after fifty years
of friendship, you'd be flinging back
confidences with brutal Tebbitry, such
Thatcherite *whose-fault-is-it-but-only-yours?*

I 'whinge', have lived too long 'in the past',
should get up off my 'lazy arse' As if
a singular effort of will is all it takes.

You're like those one-eyed evangelicals who spout
'get real', claim only *their* world's valid to be in.
And you a teacher judging me 'foetal',
infant who doesn't respond to condescensions,
must stand out in the corridor!

Well, you can stick philosophies of blame
where they belong, you're not the one
to tell me where and how to love.

Easy now for me to think of you
under some flashy cruise-ship's chandeliers,
coiffured, manicured, so *quelle finesse,*
absorbed in brochure photos of the world...
whales' tails... cocktails afterwards...

or at its stern-rails retching up the thought of me
into the pale-blue-yonder of a fading wake.

II

Go to the cave of love
And look for music in a jollier key.
                              Horace trans. James Michie

That off my chest, now it's time
to move into a milder clime –
hence this consonance of rhyme:

a lighter kind of rhetoric
than lunging with a vengeful stick
might, who knows, just do the trick.

Taking things with a pinch of salt,
trying to overlook the fault
that led to such a crass assault.

Exasperation some might feel
must be, though wrong, as palpable, as real
as heartburn after a fulsome meal.

Someone perhaps told her pay no heed,
your Simpson fellow is a weed,
let his wife and him just go to seed.

Trouble is the game
of finding someone or some thing to blame,
comes up with reasons grossly lame:

you dig out 'explanations' then decide
what one should do, all cut and dried.
Would it were that simplified!

With that dreadful pudder o'er his head,
Reason not the need, poor Lear once said.
Let's put this persiflage to bed.

Brideshead Revisited

The way to solve a problem you see in life is to
live in a way that makes the problem disappear.
                              Wittgenstein

There is doe-eyed Julia divorcing Rex,
wistful Charles divorcing frivolous Celia,
Marchmain wheezing out his wicked
deathbed masterstroke, his terrible divorce-from-life.

See how *in extremis* the Church
made shivering wimps of them, how they lit
candles, called a priest with unction, to pray
for a sign the rascally milord – even comatose –
might be contrite, make 'peace with God', be loved
forever afterwards somewhere beyond the blue beyond.
They all want to believe it 'a good and beautiful death'.

I'm not looking forward to that deadly decree absolute,
not now that I've got used to you, your ways, your decency,
and how together we fondly keep our kind of faith.

Angel of Death...

except of course it wasn't:

just a man with a black attaché case
come to help us rearrange our wills

talking matter-of-factly of being dead
and what's to be done with what of us we leave behind.

That night a demented someone else who was myself
went raging through darkness to find you

then pitching down boulder-strewn rapids

screaming

awoke.

The River on a Black Day

I

The last time I saw the estuary like this
was a wild November day, fists of wind
slamming in from a blurred North Wales,
waves in bullying mood, horizon shutting down,
gulls huddled on sandbars in what seemed like
vindictive indifference. I thought it the place
to have my ashes thrown, up into a punishing wind
or, better perhaps, poured in slow grey sift
over a ferryboat's side, with the tide slipping out,
so that my remaining particles
get washed out to sea, swirl with sand and bits of shell
down the estuary and into watery anywhere.

II

Will you be there to see me off,
braving the deck of the grumbling ferry
or leaning on rails at Otterspool Prom,
searching moodily into the clay-brown river? Or
will your old desperations keep you home
among the things that go on talking of me?

And what of you? Who'll fulfil your wish,
lugging a hold-all with your urn, swaddled in towels,
up the cold and glinting steps of a plane
scheduled for Berlin? Will they find the cemetery,
pour your ashes on the numbered plot
where the first man you ever loved is laid,
your grandfather? Look at him here, this photograph,
a silver-tached old man, at ease
with his pre-war self, a steadfast look offering securities
you have longed for, I could never absolutely give.

You in the heart of fought-over Europe,
me wafting about in the Gulf Stream,
under the old-salt gaze of seagulls, finally, fatally adrift.